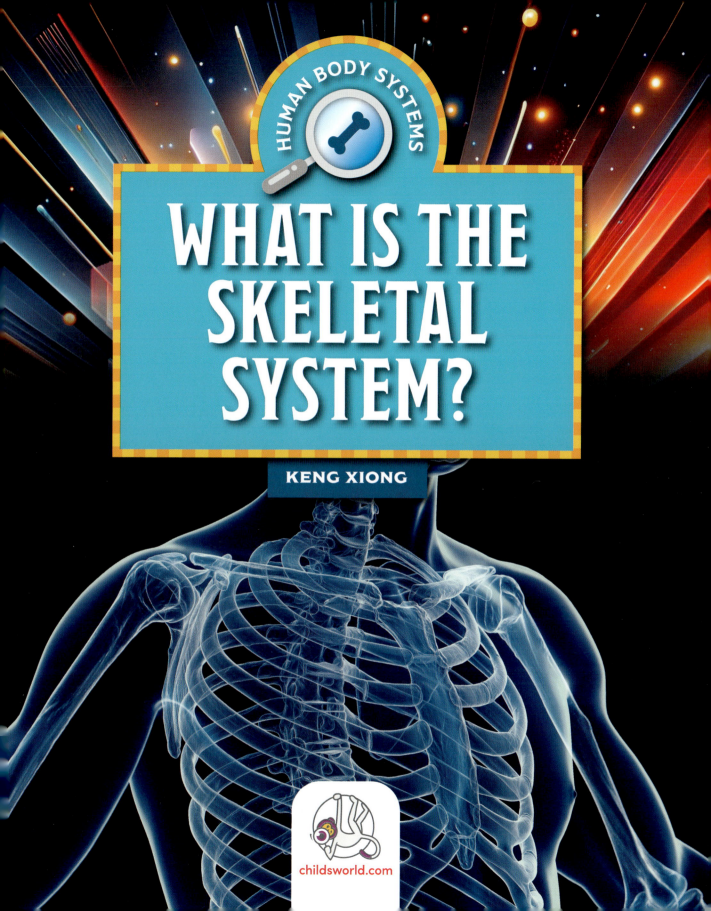

**Published by The Child's World®**
800-599-READ • www.childsworld.com

**Copyright © 2026 by The Child's World®**
All rights reserved. No part of this book may be reproduced or utilized in any form or by any means without written permission from the publisher.

**Photography Credits**
Photographs ©: Sebastian Kaulitzki/Shutterstock Images, cover (main), 1 (main); Shutterstock Images, cover (icon), 1 (icon), 3, 5, 6, 8, 9, 13, 15, 16, 17, 18–19, 20; Olga Bolbot/Shutterstock Images, 10, 22; Abramova Alena/Shutterstock Images, 11; Design elements from Shutterstock Images

**ISBN Information**
9781503871281 (Reinforced Library Binding)
9781503871632 (Portable Document Format)
9781503872875 (Online Multi-user eBook)
9781503874114 (Electronic Publication)

**LCCN** 2024951059

**Printed in the United States of America**

## About the Author
Keng Xiong is an editorial assistant from Andover, Minnesota. He has a bachelor's degree in English and creative writing. In his free time, he enjoys traveling and going to bookstores.

# TABLE OF CONTENTS

**CHAPTER 1**
## Breaking a Bone 4

**CHAPTER 2**
## The Body's Structural Support 8

**CHAPTER 3**
## Strong Bones 14

Wonder More . . . 21

Fast Facts . . . 22

Sculpting Model Skeletal Systems . . . 22

Glossary . . . 23

Find Out More . . . 24

Index . . . 24

# BREAKING A BONE

Liam put on his football helmet and walked onto the field. He was a wide receiver for his school's football team. He took a deep breath. It was the last play of the first half. He got into position, his cleats digging into the turf.

"Hike!" his quarterback yelled. Liam rushed along the sideline. He had run this route many times in practice. He turned left just as the quarterback threw the ball. It soared across the sky. Liam put out his arms and caught the ball. Cheers erupted from the bleachers. He ran down the field. The end zone was only a few yards away!

Football players often crash into each other during games. This is why it is important to wear protective gear while playing.

X-rays help doctors spot problems inside patients' bodies.

    Then a player on the other team tackled him. A loud *snap* sounded as Liam fell to the ground. He cried out as his arm flared with pain. His coaches and teammates rushed over. Liam pointed at his arm. It was clearly broken. He was placed into an ambulance.

At the hospital, Liam got an **X-ray**. It showed the bone in his arm that had broken. He would have to stop playing football until it healed. He was upset. But he knew he had to take care of his arm. The doctor put a cast and sling on his arm. These devices would make sure his broken bone did not move. This would help him heal faster. When Liam returned to school, his teammates signed his cast. That made him feel better.

The skeletal system is made up of the body's bones and connective **tissue**. These protect the **organs** inside the body. They also help people move. But things can go wrong with the skeletal system. People should do what they can to take care of their bones.

# CHAPTER 2

# THE BODY'S STRUCTURAL SUPPORT

The skeletal system gives structure to the body. It holds other body parts in place. Bones are important parts of the skeletal system. Bones are a type of hard tissue. Like most other parts of the body, bones are made of **cells.** The outer layer of a bone is the hardest. It contains calcium. This **mineral** makes bones hard and strong.

Milk and dairy products contain calcium.

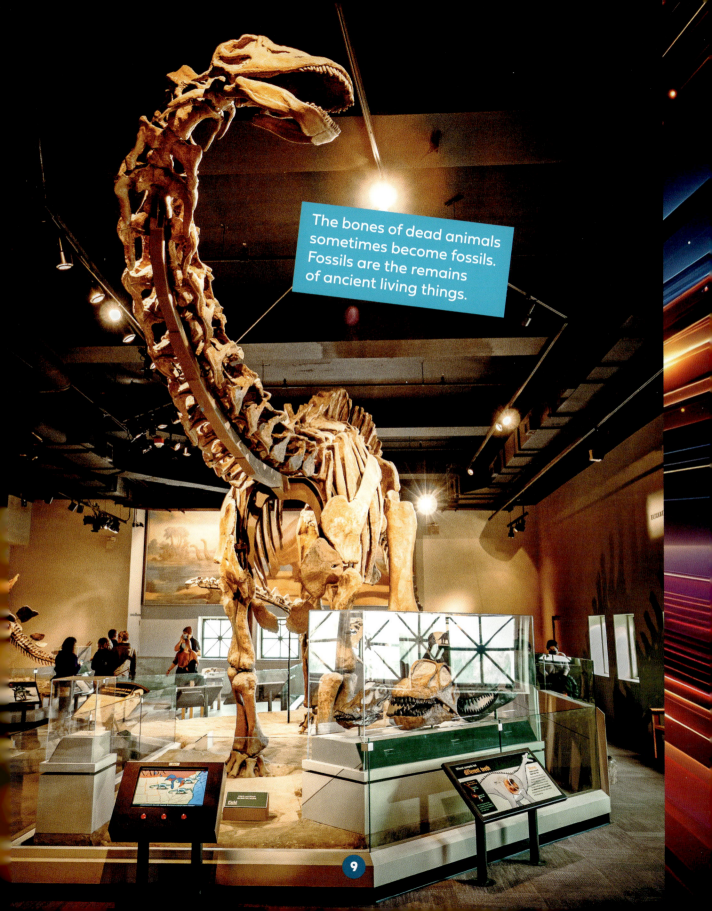

The bones of dead animals sometimes become fossils. Fossils are the remains of ancient living things.

# MAJOR BONES OF THE SKELETAL SYSTEM

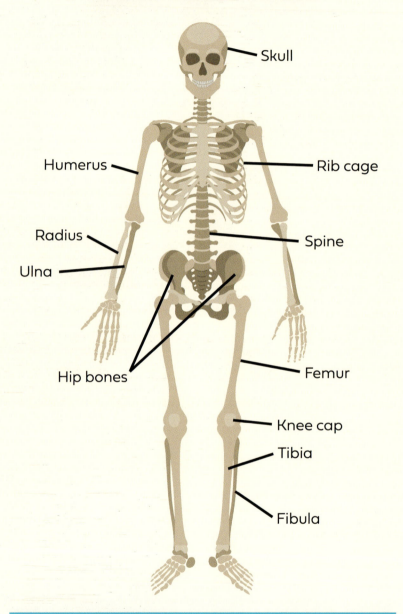

Larger body parts are usually made up of several bones. For example, the arm is made up of three main bones. They are the humerus, radius, and ulna.

Teeth and bones both contain calcium, but teeth are not bones.

Inside a bone is bone marrow. This is a soft tissue made of stem cells. Stem cells can turn into other types of cells. Some stem cells in bone marrow become blood cells. Other stem cells become bone cells and muscle cells.

Bones protect the soft organs inside the body. The rib cage protects the heart and lungs. The skull protects the brain. It also supports the muscles of the face. The spine connects the skull to the hip bones. The spine provides central support for the body. It also protects the spinal cord. This cord contains many nerves. Nerves allow the brain to control parts throughout the body.

The skeletal system also contains connective tissue. This tissue connects bones, muscles, and other body parts. Tissues that connect muscles to bones are called tendons. When people flex their muscles, tendons move bones. This allows people to move their arms, legs, and other parts.

Joints are places where two or more bones come together. Joints allow people to bend and twist body parts. Ligaments are tissues that connect bones to other bones. For example, knees and ankles are connected by ligaments.

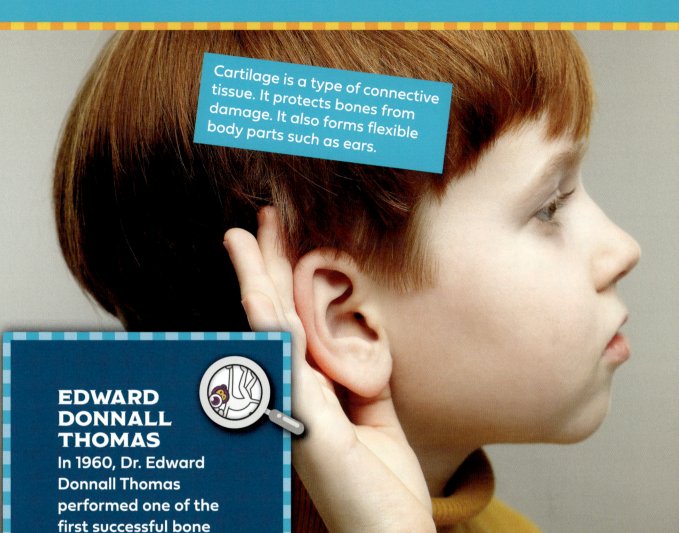

Cartilage is a type of connective tissue. It protects bones from damage. It also forms flexible body parts such as ears.

## EDWARD DONNALL THOMAS

In 1960, Dr. Edward Donnall Thomas performed one of the first successful bone marrow transplants. The patient was a child with aplastic anemia. This condition causes the bone marrow to make too few blood cells. The child received working blood cells from her identical twin. These blood cells were taken from her twin's bone marrow. In a few weeks, the patient started to recover.

# STRONG BONES

The skeletal system plays an important role in the body. Problems with the skeletal system can affect its ability to protect and support the body. It is important to take care of bones and connective tissue.

Sprains are one kind of problem that affects the skeletal system. Sprains are stretching or tearing of ligaments. These injuries take place at joints. For example, a person may cause a sprain by twisting their ankle. In many cases, the body recovers from sprains on its own. A person with a sprain should avoid overusing the injured joint while it heals.

Damage to the skeletal system can affect a person's ability to move.

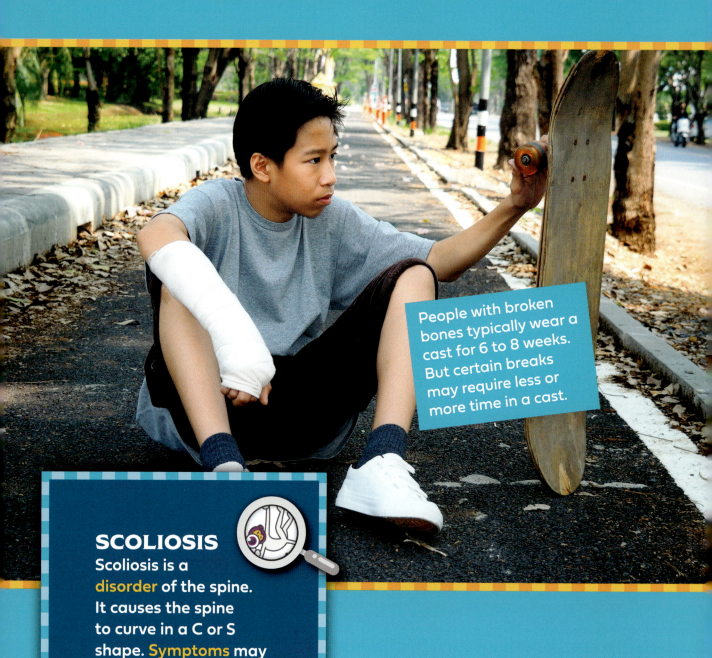

People with broken bones typically wear a cast for 6 to 8 weeks. But certain breaks may require less or more time in a cast.

## SCOLIOSIS

Scoliosis is a **disorder** of the spine. It causes the spine to curve in a C or S shape. **Symptoms** may include numbness, uneven shoulders, and an uneven waist. If the disorder progresses, it can cause back pain. Doctors can slow and correct scoliosis with surgery and other treatments.

16

Children's bones tend to heal faster than adults' bones.

Bones may break if stressed. This is called a fracture. There are many types of fractures. Fractures are either open or closed. Open fractures show bone poking through the skin. Closed fractures do not. Fractures can happen when playing sports. They can also occur in accidents such as falls.

Common symptoms after a fracture include pain and swelling. A cast or splint can help reduce pain. These devices help hold the bone in place. For some breaks, doctors may recommend surgery to help the bone heal.

Bones may also slip out of place at the joints. This is called dislocation. It can cause intense pain. A person may not be able to move. Sometimes dislocated bones go back into place on their own. But other dislocations may need to be treated by a doctor. Doctors can help put dislocated bones back into place.

There are many ways to keep the skeletal system strong. Physical activity helps strengthen muscles and bones. But it is important to protect the body when being active. Different activities require different kinds of safety gear. People should wear the recommended gear. For example, football helmets help protect the head from injury.

Car seats, booster seats, and seat belts can protect bones by reducing injuries in car crashes.

Protein is one nutrient that bones need. Foods such as fish, tofu, nuts, and asparagus are high in this nutrient.

Eating a variety of foods is also important. Different foods contain different **nutrients**. The body and its bones need a variety of nutrients to function. Foods high in calcium help bones grow and stay strong. These foods include milk products and leafy vegetables. A doctor can help a person pick the right foods for them. Doctors can also help people when they have concerns about their skeletal health.

# Wonder More

### Wondering About New Information
How much did you know about the skeletal system before reading this book? What new information did you learn? Write down three new facts that this book taught you. Was the new information surprising? Why or why not?

### Wondering How It Matters
What is one way the skeletal system relates to your life? How do you think it relates to other kids' lives? Have you or anyone you know ever broken a bone?

### Wondering Why
Joints are where two or more bones meet. The knees and elbows are examples of joints. Why does the human body have joints? What would it be like to have no knees or elbows?

### Ways to Keep Wondering
The skeletal system is one of many human body systems. After reading this book, what questions do you have about the skeletal system? What can you do to learn more about it?

# Fast Facts

- The skeletal system is made up of bones and connective tissue. The system protects the organs inside the body and helps with movement.

- Bones are made up of different types of tissue. They also hold bone marrow, which helps make blood cells and other kinds of cells.

- Things can go wrong with the skeletal system. Problems with the skeletal system can include sprains, fractures, and dislocated bones.

- There are many ways to keep the skeletal system strong. These include exercising, eating a varied diet, and seeing a doctor.

## Sculpting Model Skeletal Systems

In this activity, you will make models of the skeletal system using clay. If you do not have this material, feel free to use crayons and paper instead. This activity may be done alone or with a partner.

1. Draw an outline of the human body on a piece of paper.

2. Label bones within your outline using the following labels: rib cage, skull, leg bones, spine, arm bones. Then use the clay to sculpt each bone structure.

3. Answer the following questions: How does each bone help the body function? Select one bone and think about what would happen if it broke. How would that affect a person's daily life?

# Glossary

**cells** (SELZ) Cells are the basic units of all living things. Red blood cells are created in bone marrow.

**disorder** (diss-OR-der) A disorder is an abnormal medical condition. Scoliosis is a disorder of the spine.

**mineral** (MIN-ur-ul) A mineral is a natural, nonliving substance. Calcium is a mineral found in bones.

**nutrients** (NEW-tree-untz) Nutrients are substances in food that help the body function. Some nutrients help bones grow and stay strong.

**organs** (OR-ginz) Organs are collections of cells and tissues that work together to do a task. The skeletal system helps protect the body's organs.

**symptoms** (SIMP-tumz) Symptoms are signs of a medical condition. Some symptoms of bone fractures include pain and limited movement.

**tissue** (TIH-shyoo) Tissue is a group of similar cells that work together. Tissue connects muscles and bones.

**transplants** (TRANZ-plantz) Transplants are medical operations in which a body part is moved from its original location to a new one. One of the first successful bone marrow transplants happened in 1960.

**X-ray** (EKS-ray) An X-ray uses powerful energy to take pictures of bones and organs inside the body. An X-ray can reveal a fractured bone.

# Find Out More

## In the Library

Richmond, Marley. *What Is the Nervous System?* Parker, CO: The Child's World, 2026.

Rose, Rachel. *My Bones*. Minneapolis, MN: Bearport, 2022.

Schuh, Mari. *Sasha's Strong Skeletal System*. Minneapolis, MN: Jump!, 2022.

## On the Web

Visit our website for links about the skeletal system:

### childsworld.com/links

*Note to Parents, Caregivers, Teachers, and Librarians: We routinely verify our web links to make sure they are safe and active sites. So encourage your readers to check them out!*

# Index

bone marrow, 11, 13
broken bones, 6–7, 17

calcium, 8, 20
casts, 7, 17
connective tissues, 7, 12, 14

dislocation, 18

joints, 12, 14, 18

major bones, 10
muscles, 11–12, 18

safety gear, 4, 18
scoliosis, 16
sports, 4–7, 17–18
sprains, 14
stem cells, 11

Thomas, Edward Donnall, 13